A Chorus of Strays

A Chorus of Strays

Poems by

Roberta Schultz

© 2025 Roberta Schultz. All rights reserved.
This material may not be reproduced in any form, published,
reprinted, recorded, performed, broadcast,
rewritten, or redistributed without
the explicit permission of Roberta Schultz.
All such actions are strictly prohibited by law.

Cover design by Shay Culligan
Cover art by shndgd on Pexels
Author photo by Kevin Vance

ISBN: 978-1-63980-978-3

Kelsay Books
502 South 1040 East, A-119
American Fork, Utah 84003
Kelsaybooks.com

Dedication—

To the members of Katerina Stoykova's Poetry Boot Camp, 2024,
for all your thoughtful comments and critiques.

To Dick Hague and Sherry Cook Stanforth for
all the inspiration at Writer's Table.

And to Kari Gunter-Seymour for her Makery class.

Acknowledgments

Thank you to the following publications, in which versions of these poems previously appeared:

Common Threads: "Counterpoint," "Putnam Street Songs"
Kakalak: "Tony Bennet Sings 'Who Can I Turn To?'"
Lexington Poetry Month Anthology: "Pluck"
Lexpomo: "Pride," "Widow Skimmer," "Threat"
Pegasus: "Cedar Triptych" (2nd Place in Chaffin/Kash Poetry Prize)
Pine Mountain Sand & Gravel: Appalachian Fusion, Volume 27: "Cedar Triptych"
Verse-Virtual: "Open Me," "Cityscape," "The Orb Weaver" "I Visit Your Grave"
Yearling: "What the Heron and I Have in Common" "Swatches"

Contents

Section One: to stray means to wander

Putnam Street Songs	15
Extended Family	16
Red Tag	17
Parallel Thirds	18
Open Me	19
What the Heron and I Have in Common	20
Counterpoint	21
Salad Days	22

Section Two: to stray means to become lost

Nomad	25
Tony Bennet Sings "Who Can I Turn To?"	26
Tick Trivia as Self-Help	27
Evidence	28
Looking for India on the Way to a Nursing Home Gig	29
Threat	30
Letter from the Valley House at Loretto	31
I Visit Your Grave	32
Homophones	33

Section Three: to stray means to turn or deviate

Pluck	37
Singing Bowl	38
Not a Flood Next Time	39
a gaze blank and pitiless	41

Pride	42
The Orb Weaver	43
The Kubrick Stare	44
Widow Skimmer	45
Swatches	46

Section Four: to stray means to drift

A History of the Lake According to the Heron	49
Bongosero	51
Fall on the Ohio	52
Catch Light	53
Cedar Triptych	54
Evolution of a Knee	55
Weather Report for My State of Being	56
Sweetgrass	57
Cityscape	58

Section One: to stray means to wander

Putnam Street Songs

Then, I yowled in a chorus of strays.
We'd clasp hands and sing names at each gate—
those wrought iron and wood thresholds
we'd never dare toe our Keds across.

Each neighborhood pal had a signature tune:
The march-like cadence of *Oh, Sylvia!*
The rising tone spiral of *Oh, Roberta!*
The descending resolve in *Oh, Buddy!*

Now, we mail voices without song, search engines
with no whiff of Jack Sorrell's on-street oil change,
swipe screens where no forehead leans, thumb
phones that lack the sandbox grit of a fast grip.

Extended Family

The porch creates some kind of portal.
A thin overhang shelters our path past

>	the cellar door and the downspouts—a past
>	where we live behind our grandma's house

in a place called The Back. Not a whole house
with a bathroom and a stove. Just two rooms.

>	We curtain off the big side for two bedrooms.
>	The lesser half becomes our kitchen thanks

to the hand sink and our hotplate. Thanks
to the table and the heater, we gather

>	our small family for breakfast, but gather
>	with my grandma's brood for other meals.

She taps at her window to signal meal
time. We pass through the slim porch portal.

Red Tag

—inspired by the poem "Conduit" by Richard Hague

In winter, I mourn the death of color—one day capturing photos of a purpled wild rose stalk, so bruised by frost after a cruel January thaw. Leaves bleed out against the heft of gray. Later, outside my frosty window, one crimson salesman chatters from the pin oak branch. He sings about a bargain price for all frozen dreams:

Cheap, cheap, cheap, cheap. Ha, ha, ha, ha, ha, ha, ha, ha!
Cheap, cheap, cheap, cheap. Ha, ha, ha, ha, ha, ha, ha, ha!

Little flames crackle
steady under heavy skies.
Hearth songs warm my ears.

Parallel Thirds

When
June
begins
like a song
I have always known,
I slide beside in harmony.

Open Me

—in response to Rosemerry Wahtola Trommer's poems about opening

like a door you rush through for something you forgot
like a puzzle you've longed to work that's not too easy

like a well-wrapped present under the tree
in the shape of something you want, not need

like an envelope that looks official
awarding you the prize

like a brand new book you've been waiting to read—
not too scary, but a best-seller all the same

like a fine champagne with a rocket cork
that will blast across your sky in celebration

like a fresh box of crunchy cereal
with all the nuts and raisins plump

Open me

in these last few hours when darkness
dominates, when distant stars shine
longer than our one sun

When I open, I will share
every two-word prayer I know
for thanks

What the Heron and I Have in Common

Like me, he needs his time alone,
his long pose on one leg
at the edge of the lake's stillness.

Like me, he searches the surface
for signs, little bubbles
that sing *all will be well.*

Like him, I circle the water
to find what escapes me—
the slippery fish, the catch light.

Like him, I am wary of others
finding my sanctuary, gnawing
the bones of my treasure.

Like me, he hides behind the shagbark,
avoids intruder traipse
into his peace, onto his plan.

Like me, he bellows prehistoric squawk
when surprised, when confronted,
flaps away to higher perch.

Like him, I reflect
on every rippled mirror,
expect something shiny will rise.

Like him, I gather stems
to plump my nest, to comfort
those who wait at rest for my scent.

Though framed in leaves, we see each other
clear, nod our gawky greetings, necks
curved close to our breasts.

Counterpoint

Through the screen door, I hear
        a flicker chisel at the porch bannister.

At first I mistake her for a jackhammer, some ardent
        workman digging up the nearby asphalt lane.

But then I see her hang upside down from the rail
        tapping for some hollow spot to pack with sticks

and broom sedge. Maybe she feels the succulent
        buzz of dinner inside the wooden trim—fat bees

carpenter and dive bomb anyone who dares
        venture onto slender planks for sun.

All day they drone duet—bumble
        and hum, hammer and drill. Nesting

and feeding, feeding and nesting until
        night breaks into shrill nocturne.

Salad Days

deer
next to the woods

parsley
seasoned with frost

grass
drizzled fresh green

path
for irresistible graze

Section Two: to stray means to become lost

Nomad

What does he escape from, plod toward?
        A three-foot long Sulcata tortoise breaststrokes

down our gravel road.
        Maybe the wide expanse of green

so unlike any scene he's known so far.
        No bars, no fence, no wilted lettuce

slime on a slick cage floor.
        No winter shed with low light and little heat.

No shrinking into shadow until someone
        remembers to share the sun.

Maybe the craggy locust resembles
        trees from the Sahel or Serengeti.

Maybe the dust under pebbles
        promises sand. One lone Saharan

wanders this clay Kentucky hill.
        How will he survive?

I bring him collards from the garden.
        I swear, he might be smiling.

His eager neck stretches
        toward tender stems.

As he nibbles gently, I trace the pointy armor
        on his hard shell home.

Tony Bennet Sings "Who Can I Turn To?"

on Ed Sullivan, March 21, 1965

Belly down on the knotty pine floor,
I face the darkness of questions.

>Dark are the songs that end with questions.
>Pencil and paper in front of me, ready.

To write down every word, my hands so ready.
So keen to capture the lyrics' rhythm.

>Crescendoes of pain roar under the rhythm.
>I open, startled from jagged rocking.

The Stones and The Supremes rule charts of rock,
but I navigate Sunday night by show tunes.

>Marchers in Selma stomp spiritual tunes
>while astronauts pace the silence in space.

I scribe unanswered cries on white space,
belly down on the knotty pine floor.

Tick Trivia as Self-Help

We climb the highway hill
where teasel remnants spring.
Our stalkers never jump or drop
as is the popular notion.

Instead, they cling to slim dead sprigs
by their third and fourth pairs of legs.
They hold those first pairs outstretched,
questing to grasp a passing host.

My beagle's breath, my lack
of deodorant, our collective body heat,
our stomping vibrations through brush—
all signals to latch on by static electric path.

Later, I'm horrified at red carnage
in a cat scratch, a feeding pool gash
where the hypostome injects my skin
with inhibitors, slows new wounds from healing.

Evidence

A hornet's nest torn so open in winter
causes me to wonder at desperate feats.

> Bears can stretch for out-of-reach treats on their feet.
> But, this home sways near the maple tree top.

Bears would need to climb close to thin top
branches, stretch out length-wise, swipe and claw,

> sending the whole abode crashing to ground. Claws
> might then peel back paper and spear all the food—

frozen larvae and hollow wasp husks. Mute food
whose stillness fuels the hungry living.

> Once abuzz, now suspended. No living
> creature claims what's left through shredded edges.

My guess? Cold and hurried squirrels or flickers edged
this hornet's nest—so torn, so open in winter.

Looking for India on the Way to a Nursing Home Gig

Would GPS have helped Columbus?
My sister sits in the back seat.
Her phone doles out directions.

In 500 feet, turn right.

Of course, Vickie ignores her.
I used to print out detailed directions
for every gig. We almost never got lost.

These days, in some kind of explorer
mindset, Vickie turns right
on a whim.

You were supposed to do that in 500 feet.
Violet reminds her.

I think I know a shortcut.

I say nothing.
I am a dinosaur
who still believes
that looking at a map
or reading over directions
might be helpful
to get somewhere
we intend.

Recalculating, drones the phone voice.

We are never going to find the spices of India.
But we're sure to unnerve indigenous folks
by claiming they are Indians.

Threat

Great
blue
heron
glides over
glassy lake surface.
All stillness fractured for the fish.

Letter from the Valley House at Loretto

I am writing you from across the pasture,
    you, atop the hill where the rows are even

and well-trimmed. I, down here where all
    the pieces tumble to their final use.

The strange hospital lamp, the TV stand
    from 1972, a recliner like my mom used

to own with the side wooden handle
    that springs all unsuspecting loungers upright

with a sudden jolt. None of the curtains
    match. The living room tables, too tall

for their chairs. Every scrap repurposed.
    Did I tell you how kind it was

for you to come to one of my first readings
    in that neighborhood bar courtyard?

You slipped in quietly, took a seat near the street,
    so I didn't see you until I was leaving.

Did I tell you how kind it was for you to say
    I came just to hear you?

I Visit Your Grave

in this solace you guided me toward
after other adventures on switchbacks
through mountains. We laughed
about how wrong Mapquest
got it. State park hosts gaped
at our dangerous route.
No one takes that
road!

And now, after turns we could not
have guessed, you are buried
here at this haven, younger
than I am, too soon.
I notice tributes
scattered over
other stones,
wonder what
I can offer.
Just this—

written on a leathery bouquet
of fallen gingko
leaves—

my poem about how you
opened arms and
heart, led me
safe into
sacred
space.

Homophones

Simone tried to practice her English on us.
All the cousins did except Raymonde who gushed
wild pantomime along with her French,
so that even I—a first-time visitor—might grasp.

*Stay with us for two weeks, and you too
will speak French.*

She added pats on my back,
aimed points at my mouth,
raised two arthritic digits
in the air for emphasis.

But Simone gathered my hands
after midi to pull me to my feet
in blunt Anglo-Saxon—

First we ate, now we sing.

A little puzzled at this custom
after the many-coursed meal,

I stepped deliberately with her
into La Celle St. Cloud afternoons
to walk and walk and walk—*balade.*

We stomped little songs to scatter the birds.
Wings lifted our percussive ballads
beyond all translation.

Section Three: to stray means to turn or deviate

Pluck

How
hard
to break
silences
with nothing but your
faith that the string will still vibrate.

Singing Bowl

She appears before the mirror clearly
overdressed for the bagels and coffee bash.

> We poets charge, armed with nouns and verbs to bash
> paths toward a gut punch poem's last line—

a gasp-for-air or rasp-in-rapture last line.
No ripple-on-water breath allowed.

> No rustle of silky kimono aloud.
> No rising chorus of temple bell chimes.

One mallet circles the metal rim, but chimes
no jarring peal of awakening here.

> A spiral siren winds ballads. Hear
> overtones grind in praise of around.

Her song—wound with wounds—echoes in rounds
that ring beneath the mirror's clarity.

Not a Flood Next Time

Well, well, well. Weren't we the little bummers
at the Starlight Teenage 4H Club? What with Dale
trying to convince freshmen girls to sink drowsy
heads into his heather sweater for a prolonged
slow dance to the Beach Boys' "In My Room."

Like stopwatches, syncopated ping pong
clicks cadenced through any silence
where we might seize our chance,
guitars slung, to fill the void
with folk scare:

"The Times They are a Changin"
"Springfield Mining Disaster"
"Wasn't That a Time?"
"Well, Well, Well."

Dale turned up the stereo, dropping
the tone arm needle gently
onto sleepy, scratchy ballads.

Mark, Gary and I leaned on the edge
of the couch, ready to rise if the rabble
needed rousing. They didn't care.
They still don't.

It's hard to stand alert for years, lyrics
firing neurons in a mostly intact brain
with such clear and present
certainty:

Come gather round, people.
Isn't this a terrible time?
God said a fire, not
a flood— in a world
that's never seen
sun nor sky.

a gaze blank and pitiless

—from The Second Coming, William Butler Yeats

blinks from the face.
Sounds garble and bubble
from gasping fish lips.
Hands chop out parentheses
in air space that narrows, widens,
then narrows again. Hands pull
at margins of an open blue coat,
jerk opposing edges down, tug
all hems toward closing.

This one will claim to know you.
This one will promise to fight your fight.
This one slouches in shades of chaos,
darks out the desert sun.

Pride

June
has
rainbowed
all over
dull stuck-in-mud fields.
(Gardens blush in bud, then in bloom.)
Brighter hues bruise new horizons
long shaded in clouds
and shadow.
Brilliance
won't
hide.

The Orb Weaver

sets her strands
   in a tight net
that spans our basement door.

She calculates our comings
   and goings each morning.
How many generations

could she feed
   from such a catch?
My forehead bursts

through slender silk. I brush
   away her wispy weave.
Undaunted, she patterns on.

Oh, how she dreams.
She dreams.

The Kubrick Stare

Those dead eyes lunge
at the viewer straight
from the heart
of darkness.

He tilts his head down,
glares into the camera—
a signal to the nervous
movie fan that something
horrible is about to happen
in this script where one
character has reached
the apex of derangement:

chopping through the door
with an axe, *Honey, I'm home!*

        seething through his mouth's red slash,
        why so serious?

              hissing through the bars.
              Clarice.

We're not talking about director's cut.
Just one last threatening slice
by Kurtz from *Apocalypse Now*.

He wants to rip the guts
from every opponent,

fling them—twisted and dripping
with ketchup like his dinner—
at walls of his own making.

Widow Skimmer

Male
leaves
female
by herself
after mating time.
Under warm ripples, she tubes broods
unguarded by father's wing bands.
He skims the surface
unbound by
widow's
black
veil.

Swatches

—an ekphrastic poem inspired by Mark Rothko's oil painting,
   Untitled (Red, Orange)

Blocked out on top is the color of ache. I make its pulsing blood from pigments and powders. Tinctures can't cure, but when cast on canvas from a certain distance, hues reveal flickers of light, sparks to ignite each tight twitch in a terrified chest.

Beneath the red, I brush pale orange blush of a monk's robe. A slender map that mutes all syncopated pounding in my ears from drums of doubt:

You are always wrong.
You were never an artist.
Here hangs the raw truth.

Section Four: to stray means to drift

A History of the Lake According to the Heron

There was always a gorge—
a deep wound in the downward slant
toward the river.

The water always poured down
over the highland fields, down
the cowpaths, to the Licking.

But no fish here until
Farmer John built a clay dam
on the steep crest of hill.

He asked The State to help him stock.
He promised his neighbors
the right to fish

for bluegill and bass.
That's when my father
found our hole.

Our perch in the shagbark
with the best sight lines
for ripples and rise.

We left the colony trees to the rest of our kind,
found the fattest bass, unending
swarms of bluegill.

And feeder fish for snacks.
The new owners stock themselves.
No competition from human neighbors.

Sometimes I forget why I came—
the breeze so easy, the trees
so lush with leaves.

But then, I hear the far-off squawk from my mate
at the river, imagine little rumbles
of hunger.

I fish.
I fish.
I fish.

I pose motionless on one leg when
the woman and the beagle
ramble around the path.

Into the slant of evening,
I fish.

Bongosero

In the heaviness
of this weighty day
when steel wool
barbells the sky,

I tap out a pulse
on the macho, hope
I can tone the hembra
for offbeats, lead

our ready circle into
the heat of habanera—
a rhythm that sings its name
below, so fingers can dance above.

Fall on the Ohio

Outside the window
  scumbles blur

Impressionistic brush strokes
  from a spare palate.

Reds and browns
  fog against the silver river.

Power lines etch thin divisions
  to part the plane.

The sky—awash in gray—shines
  behind steel wool.

Catch Light

Lean into the darkness of this day.
That's where you might find deeper reflection.

>Liminal and still, light leaks from reflective
>lens of lake and pool of sky, captured in eye

for a second's wink. My blinking eye
focuses, washes clear and open.

>A dim palate of gray-green and white opens
>to the possibility of gold ghosts.

Trampled patches of broom sedge echo the ghost
soak of grass dried in fall's fiery rays.

>Through my humble camera, distorted rays
>mimic how sun bounces off cedars.

Swaddled thick in the wool of clouds, cedars
seem to lean into the darkness of this day.

Cedar Triptych

Across:

We stand/shoulder to shoulder/above the whine of sirens/along the highway hills/like empaneled judges/we watch the traffic river/green witness to rush—/we hold silent court/as judgment passes slowly/our roots tuck sideways/edge the Bradford Pears/here on this steep bluff/between loose rocks/(who never wait their turn)/we set our bond

Down:

We stand
along highway hills,
green witness to rush—
our roots tuck sideways
between loose rocks

shoulder to shoulder
like empaneled judges
we hold silent court
edge the Bradford Pears
(who never wait their turn)

above the whine of sirens
we watch the traffic river
as judgment passes slowly
here on this steep bluff
we set our bond

Evolution of a Knee

When it buckled the first time I stood
and dumped me onto my diapered butt.

When it banged on the steel cellar door,
the concrete sidewalk, the iron gate when

my skittering feet, skidding bike, and
sliding skateboard would not stop.

When the growing pains would ache
at night in every nerve and joint.

Still, I could bend to pet heads, kneel
to say prayers, bounce back to upright,
and run.

When it buckled the last time I stood
and dumped me onto my butt again.

When the growing pain groans
night and day in every nerve and joint.

When bouncing back to upright
involves two hands and a grunt.

Pet heads stretch up to reach my touch.
I'm mindful of the chair underneath
each prayer.

Weather Report for My State of Being

Partly centered tonight
with breeze in the treetops.

Expect occasional katydids
with light, scattered peepers.

In-the-moment showers arrive
overnight along with measurable

accumulation of autumn olive berries.
Thick drifts of vanilla yogurt follow.

70% chance of downy by morning
as silky extends into late afternoon.

A weekend cool front promises
mostly gray-green waves of calm

with dense creamsicle patches
and slowly dissipating Shiraz.

Sweetgrass

My hair combusts like the fine white frizz left by thistle.
      Spent blooms nod, reflect on sun's simmer.
            Curious crow steals seared shimmer
                  to thread her nest.

I taste bitter hips of wild rose, zest of autumn olive.
      Shagbark nut butters my tongue as I tug silver wisps
            from the corner of my mouth, slide bent fingers
                  down slick strands.

Divide silk in three parts, with worry doll weaving.
      Vanilla smoke curls from a river shell
            as braids burn clean
                  from the fire.

Cityscape

I can't stop writing this poem—
the one where I plunge into memory's
sinkhole and land on the broken stone steps
at the school where my mother learns numbers.

I can't stop writing this poem—
the one where we sing "Goodnight, Irene"
on the front stoop while streetlights sizzle
moths into brighter gravity.

I can't stop writing this poem—
the one where concrete smells of salt
after rain. Downpours stream dead leaves
toward metal sewer lids. Like ancient coins,

they adorn each corner, swallow the gutter
swell under Putnam. Waterfalls gush
toward the Licking, hushed only
by the rumbling rush of passenger trains.

Whistles wail us from bunkbed dreams.
Above the tracks, the windows
of 13th Street wink out
like dying stars.

About the Author

A Chorus of Strays is Roberta Schultz's seventh collection of poetry. Three of her chapbooks were published by Finishing Line Press while a fourth chapbook, *Asking Price,* was chosen by Workhorse Writers for their 2022 series. *Underscore,* her first full-length collection, was published by Dos Madres Press in 2022. *Deep Ends,* published in January 2025 by Finishing Line Press, is her second full-length collection.

Songwriter and poet, Roberta has had work appear in *Women Speak, Vol.7-10, Persimmon Tree, Sheila-Na-Gig, Panoplyzine, Riparian, Pine Mountain Sand & Gravel, Kakalak, Let Me Say This* (a poetry anthology with Dolly Parton as the main theme), and other anthologies.

She leads drum circles and serves as an Arts in Healing musician.

www.ingramcontent.com/pod-product-compliance
Lightning Source LLC
Chambersburg PA
CBHW030915170426
43193CB00009BA/858